The
SPIRIT of
LOVING

D1009933

The
SPIRIT of
LOVING

Compiled & Edited by
EMILY HILBURN SELL

SHAMBHALA
Boston & London
1995

Shambhala Publications, Inc.
Horticultural Hall
300 Massachusetts Avenue
Boston, Massachusetts 02115

9   8   7   6   5   4   3   2   1
First Edition
Printed in the United States of America on acid-free paper ♾
Distributed in the United States by Random House, Inc.,
and in Canada by Random House of Canada Ltd

Library of Congress Cataloging-in-Publication Data

The spirit of loving/compiled and edited by Emily Hilburn Sell.
    p.   cm.   ISBN 1-57062-076-8 (pbk.: alk. paper)
        1. Love.   I. Sell, Emily Hilburn.
        BF575.L8S64   1995   94-22605
        152.4′1—dc20   CIP

For David—beloved—
and his cousins
Ben, Sloan, Will, Jordan, Max, Anne, and Emily.
Blessed by love from birth,
may you master the art and practice it widely.

THE DAY WILL COME WHEN, after harnessing the winds, the tides, and gravitation, we shall harness for God the energies of love. And on that day, for the second time in the history of the world, man will have discovered fire.

— PIERRE TEILHARD DE CHARDIN

CONTENTS

ACKNOWLEDGMENTS

IN COMPILING THIS BOOK,
I have enjoyed the support of my husband, John, whose physical absence while I was working on this project informed my passion for it; and my friends at Shambhala Publications, whose insight and integrity have so brightened the world of late-twentieth-century publishing: Sam and Hazel Bercholz, Dan Barrett, Brian Boland, Kendra Crossen, Jacquie Giorgi, Jonathan Green, David O'Neal, Jennifer Pursley, Jean Stewart, Peter Turner—whose editorial acumen has enriched this book—and others whom I have yet to meet. I also wish to thank my family for the early circle of love, as well as Chögyam Trungpa, Rinpoche, whose teachings have opened so many hearts.

PREFACE

LOVE AND RELATIONSHIP
are universally experienced aspects of everyday life that can
lead to either attachment or liberation. This book celebrates
their liberating quality. Here short selections from the works
of philosophers, psychologists, and spiritual teachers describe
the many ways in which love and relationship can help us
awaken to our own inherent freedom as human beings. Inter-
spersed among these selections are short excerpts from fiction that evoke the experience of love. (My apologies to the
poets and songwriters, who deserve books of their own!)
While my intent in compiling this book has been to provide
inspiration—not a survey of views on love from every time
and place—the selections range from the words of the early
philosophers on love to those of contemporary psychothera-
pists on relationship, from the Christian mystics to the Buddhist and Taoist sages.

Love is a force that connects us to every strand of the
universe, an unconditional state that characterizes human
nature, a form of knowledge that is always there for us if
only we can open ourselves to it. Relationship is condi-
tional upon an object. It is a form of skillful means through
which we can cultivate patience, generosity, discipline, integrity, and many other virtues in our daily lives.

The liberating potential of love and relationship has many facets. For example, love and relationship can operate as a mysterious source of growth. They offer us a glimpse of the absolute, as well as the opportunity to open ourselves to it. Through them, we can learn to let go. They are the gateway to discovering the importance of "other" above "self." In the same vein, they are great unifiers and opportunities for self-knowledge and inner work. They have healing power. They help us to dance in the present moment.

It is my hope that reading this little book will provoke thought, inspire feeling, and elucidate the serious yet playful matter of love and relationship. Yet the best knowledge of the subject comes from practicing it oneself. Therefore, tongue in cheek, I advise the reader to heed Krishnamurti's words:

> Put away the book, the description, the tradition, the authority, and take the journey of self-discovery. Love, and don't be caught in opinions and ideas about what love is or should be. When you love, everything will come right. Love has its own action. Love, and you will know the blessings of it. Keep away from the authority who tells you what love is and what it is not. No authority knows and he who knows cannot tell. Love, and there is understanding.

E. H. S.
Halifax, Nova Scotia | *May 1994*

The
SPIRIT of
LOVING

EROS, THE GOD OF LOVE, emerged to create the earth. Before, all was silent, bare, and motionless. Now all was life, joy, and motion.

— EARLY GREEK MYTH

Love is a relationship between things that live, holding them together in a sort of unison. There are other vital relationships. But love is this special one.

In every living thing there is the desire for love, or for the relationship of unison with the rest of things. That a tree should desire to develop itself between the power of the sun, and the opposite pull of the earth's centre, and to balance itself between the four winds of heaven, and to unfold itself between the rain and the shine, to have roots and feelers in blue heaven and innermost earth, both, this is a manifestation of love: a knitting together of the diverse cosmos into a oneness, a tree.

— D. H. LAWRENCE

LOVE IS THE MOST UNI-
versal, the most tremendous and the most mysterious of
the cosmic forces.

— PIERRE TEILHARD DE CHARDIN

LOVE . . . IS UNIVERSALLY acknowledged to be among the oldest of things. And in addition to this, Love is the author of our greatest advantages; for I cannot imagine a greater happiness and advantage to one who is in the flower of youth than an amiable lover, or to a lover, than an amiable object of his love. For neither birth, nor wealth, nor honours, can awaken in the minds of men the principles which should guide those who from their youth aspire to an honourable and excellent life, as Love awakens them.

— PLATO

In reality love is a *cosmic phenomenon,* in which men, humanity, are merely accidents: a cosmic phenomenon which has nothing to do with either the lives or the souls of men, any more than because the sun is shining, by its light men may go about their little affairs, and may utilize it for their own purposes. If men would only understand this, even with a part of their consciousness, a new world would open, and to look on life from all our usual angles would become very strange.

For then they would understand that love is something else, and of quite a different order from the petty phenomena of earthly life.

— P. D. OUSPENSKY

LOVE IS A VERY IMPOR-
tant matter in life. Nobody can ignore it. In general . . .
love can be classified into two different categories: broad
love and narrow love. Broad love is humanistic, and all
the ancient sages were recognized for their broad love.
Confucius (551–479 BCE) and Mencius (372–298 BC)
exalted humanistic love. Mo Tzu (501–416 BC) exalted
universal love and made himself as a model to realize it.
He led a life of absolute self-abnegation. He exerted
himself to the fullest extent of his life by working for
the peace of humanity. Lao Tzu valued natural impartial
love as the highest level. Śakyamuni exalted compassion
and equal love. In general, humanistic love is developed,
peaceful, impersonal and dispassionate love. This is what
human nature was born with and what human beings
should continue to cultivate. Also, in general, narrow
love can only be practiced between two people, like a
boy and a girl, a man and a woman, a husband and wife,
or among a group of people like a family, a circle of
friends, a religious fellowship, a society, a nation or a
race.

— HUA-CHING NI

LOVE IS A SACRED RESERVE
of energy; it is like the blood of spiritual evolution.

— PIERRE TEILHARD DE CHARDIN

BELIEF IN THE EXISTENCE
of other human beings as such is love.

— W. H. AUDEN

WHEN WE SPEAK OF LOVE, we are not speaking simply of a state of mind but rather of a state of our underlying suchness. Love is not what we become but who we already are.

— STEPHEN LEVINE

I HAVE AGAIN AND AGAIN
been faced with the mystery of love, and have never
been able to explain what it is. . . . Here is the greatest
and smallest, the remotest and nearest, the highest and
lowest, and we cannot discuss one side of it without also
discussing the other. No language is adequate to this
paradox. Whatever one can say, no words express the
whole. To speak of partial aspects is always too much or
too little, for only the whole is meaningful. Love "bears
all things"; and "endures all things" (1 Cor. 13:7).
These words say all there is to be said; nothing can be
added to them. For we are in the deepest sense the
victims and the instruments of cosmogonic "love." I put
the word in quotation marks to indicate that I do not
use it in its connotation of desiring, preferring, favoring,
wishing, and similar feelings, but as something superior
to the individual, a unified and undivided whole. Being
a part, man cannot grasp the whole. He is at its mercy.
He may assent to it, or rebel against it; but he is always
caught up by it and enclosed within light and his dark-
ness, whose end he cannot see. "Love ceases not"—
whether he speaks with the "tongues of angels," or with

scientific exactitude traces the life of the cell down to its uttermost source. Man can try to name love, showering upon it all the names at his command, and still he will involve himself in endless self-deceptions. If he possesses a grain of wisdom, he will lay down his arms and name the unknown by the more unknown, *ignotum per ignotius*—that is, by the name of God. That is a confession of his subjection, his imperfection, and his dependence; but at the same time a testimony to his freedom to choose between truth and error.

— CARL GUSTAV JUNG

LOVE SEEMS TO ME . . .
A divinity the most beautiful and the best of all, and the author to all others of the excellencies with which his own nature is endowed. Nor can I restrain the poetic enthusiasm which takes possession of my discourse, and bids me declare that Love is the divinity who creates peace among men, and calm upon the sea, the windless silence of storms, repose and sleep in sadness. Love divests us of all alienation from each other, and fills our vacant hearts with overflowing sympathy; he gathers us together in such social meetings as we now delight to celebrate, our guardian and our guide in dances, and sacrifices, and feast.

— PLATO

There is hardly any word which is more ambiguous and confusing than the word "love." It is used to denote almost every feeling short of hate and disgust. It comprises everything from the love for ice cream to the love for a symphony, from mild sympathy to the most intense feeling of closeness. People feel they love if they have "fallen for" somebody. They call their dependence love, and their possessiveness too. They believe, in fact, that nothing is easier than to love, that the difficulty lies in finding the right object, and that their failure to find happiness in love is due to their bad luck in not finding the right partner. But contrary to all this confused and wishful thinking, love is a very specific feeling; and while every human being has a capacity for love, its realization is one of the most difficult achievements.

— ERICH FROMM

FIRST OF ALL, LOVE IS A joint experience between two persons—but the fact that it is a joint experience does not mean that it is a similar experience to the two people involved. There are the lover and the beloved, but these two come from different countries. Often the beloved is only a stimulus for all the stored-up love which has lain quiet within the lover for a long time hitherto. And somehow every lover knows this. He feels in his soul that his love is a solitary thing. He comes to know a new, strange loneliness and it is this knowledge which makes him suffer. So there is only one thing for the lover to do. He must house his love within himself as best he can; he must create for himself a whole new inward world—a world intense and strange, complete in himself. Let it be added here that this lover about whom we speak need not necessarily be a young man saving for a wedding ring—this lover can be man, woman, child, or indeed any human creature on this earth.

— CARSON McCULLERS

Love is so simple.

— JACQUES PRÉVERT

Directly one looked up and saw them, what she called "being in love" flooded them. They became part of that unreal but penetrating and exciting universe which is the world seen through the eyes of love. The sky stuck to them; the birds sang through them. And, what was even more exciting, she felt, too, as she saw Mr Ramsay bearing down and retreating, and Mrs Ramsay sitting with James in the window and the cloud moving and the tree bending, how life, from being made up of little separate incidents which one lived one by one, became curled and whole like a wave which bore one up with it and threw one down with it, there, with a dash on the beach.

— VIRGINIA WOOLF

LOVE IS CREATION RAISED
raised to a higher degree.

— TOYOHIKO KAGAWA

THE YOUNG WOMAN WHOM
you see is Love. She has her tent in eternity. For when
God wanted to create the world, God bent down with
the most tender love. God provided for everything that
was necessary, just like a parent who prepares an inheri-
tance for a son and with the zeal of love makes all of her
possessions available. For in all its varieties and forms,
creation recognized its Creator. For it was love which
was the source of this creation in the beginning when
God said: "Let it be!" And it was. As though in the
blinking of an eye, the whole creation was formed
through love.

The young woman is radiant in such a clear, light-
ninglike brilliance of countenance that you can't fully
look at her. That is because the fear of the Lord is repre-
sented there in such clear judgment that mortal beings
don't have the power to advance towards her without
inhibition. She wears a robe whiter than snow and more
shining than the stars. For without deception and in the
white radiance of innocence, Love embraces everything
in the saints with bright-shining works. She also wears
shoes of purest gold. For Love walks on ways that for

the best part belong to the choice of God. She holds the sun and moon in her right hand and embraces them tenderly. For the right hand of God embraces all creatures and is especially extended over peoples, kingdoms, and all goods. . . . The whole creation calls this maiden "Lady." For it was from her that all of creation proceeded, since Love was the first. She made everything.

— HILDEGARD OF BINGEN

DRIVEN BY THE FORCES of love, the fragments of the world seek each other so that the world may come to being.

— PIERRE TEILHARD DE CHARDIN

LOVE IS FOR CREATION; and if creation is not possible, then for procreation; and if even that is not possible, then for creations of which, perhaps fortunately, we are unconscious. Take it, however, as the fundamental truth about Love: that it always creates.

— A. R. ORAGE

MAN'S CREATIVE STRUGGLE,
his search for wisdom and truth, is a love story.

— IRIS MURDOCH

IN ALL LIVING NATURE
(and perhaps also in that which we consider as dead)
love is the motive force which drives the creative activity
in the most diverse directions.

— P. D. OUSPENSKY

MY HEART WILL ALWAYS fly to you like a bird, from any place on earth, and it will surely find you . . . that you had become so much a part of the Heaven that stretches above me that I had only to raise up my eyes to be by your side. And even if they flung me into a dungeon, that piece of Heaven would still spread out within me and my heart would fly up to it like a bird, and that is why everything is so simple, so terribly simple and beautiful and full of meaning.

— ETTY HILLESUM

THE SIGHT OF ANYTHING
extremely beautiful, in nature or in art, brings back the
memory of what one loves, with the speed of lightning.
That is, . . . all that is beautiful and sublime in the world
takes part in the beauty of what one loves, and this unexpected glimpse of happiness immediately fills the eyes
with tears. This is how love of the beautiful and love
give each other life.

— STENDHAL

WHAT IN COMMON LAN-
guage we call beauty, which is in harmony of lines, col-
ors, sounds, or in grouping of words or thoughts, delights us only because we cannot help admitting a truth
in it that is ultimate. "Love is enough," the poet has
said; it carried its own explanation, the joy of which can
only be expressed in a form of art which also has that
finality. Love gives evidence to something which is outside us but which intensely exists and thus stimulates
the sense of our own existence. It radiantly reveals the
reality of its objects, though these may lack qualities that
are valuable or brilliant.

— RABINDRANATH TAGORE

HE WHO IS IN LOVE IS wise and is becoming wiser, sees newly every time he looks at the object beloved, drawing from it with his eyes and his mind those virtues it possesses.

— RALPH WALDO EMERSON

Let a lover's mind work for twenty-four hours, and this is what you will find: In the salt mines of Salzburg, one tosses, in the abandoned depths of the mine, a tree branch that winter has stripped of leaves; two or three months later one retrieves it covered with brilliant crystallizations; the smallest branches, those no thicker than a titmouse's foot, are adorned with an infinity of diamonds, ever-changing, dazzling; one can no longer recognize the original branch. What I call crystallization is that mental process that draws from whatever presents itself the discovery that the loved object has new perfections.

— STENDHAL

LOVE BRINGS THE REAL, and not just the ideal, vision of what others are because it is a glimpse of what we are bodily. For what is ordinarily called the body is an abstraction. It is the conventional fiction of an object seen apart from its relation to the universe, without which it has no reality whatsoever. But the mysterious and unsought uprising of love is the experience of complete relationship with another, transforming our vision not only of the beloved but of the whole world.

— ALAN WATTS

LOVE IS THE EXTREMELY difficult realisation that something other than oneself is real. Love, and so art and morals, is the discovery of reality.

— IRIS MURDOCH

THERE IS BUT ONE POS-
sible way in which human elements, innumerably diverse
by nature, can love one another: it is by knowing themselves all to be centred upon a single "super-centre"
common to all, to which they can only attain, each at
the extreme of himself, through their unity.

— PIERRE TEILHARD DE CHARDIN

Every true deed is a loving deed. All true deeds arise from contact with a beloved thing and flow into the universe. Any true deed brings, out of lived unity, unity into the world. Unity is not a property of the world, but its task. To form unity out of the world is our never-ending work.

— MARTIN BUBER

TO LOVE OUR NEIGHBOR
as ourselves does not mean that we should love all people equally, for I do not have an equal love for all the modes of existence of myself. Nor does it mean that we should never make them suffer, for I do not refuse to make myself suffer. But we should have with each person the relationship of one conception of the universe to another conception of the universe, and not to a part of it.

— W. H. AUDEN

IF YOU LOVE YOURSELF, you love everybody else as you do yourself. As long as you love another person less than you love yourself, you will not really succeed in loving yourself, but if you love all alike, including yourself, you will love them as one person and that person is both God and man. Thus he is a great and righteous person who, loving himself, loves all others equally.

— MEISTER ECKHART

Even under the irresistible compulsion of the pressures causing it to unite, Mankind will only find and shape itself if men can learn to love one another in the very act of drawing closer.

— PIERRE TEILHARD DE CHARDIN

LOVE FOR MAN CANNOT be separated from the love for one individual. To love one person productively means to be related to his human core, to him as representing mankind. Love for one individual, in so far as it is divorced from love for man, can refer only to the superficial and to the accidental; of necessity it remains shallow. While it may be said that love for man differs from motherly love inasmuch as the child is helpless and our fellow men are not, it may also be said that even this difference exists only in relative terms. All men are in need of help and depend on one another. Human solidarity is the necessary condition for the unfolding of any one individual.

— ERICH FROMM

YOU ARE WORKING FOR the whole, you are acting for the future. Seek no reward, for great is your reward on this earth: the spiritual joy which is only vouchsafed to the righteous man. Fear not the great nor the mighty, but be wise and ever serene. Know the measure, know the times, study that. When you are left alone, pray. Love to throw yourself on the earth and kiss it. Kiss the earth and love it with an unceasing, consuming love. Love all men, love everything. Seek that rapture and ecstasy. Water the earth with the tears of your joy and love those tears. Don't be ashamed of that ecstasy, prize it, for it is a gift of God and a great one.

— FYODOR DOSTOEVSKY

THE UNITY OF ALL EXISTENCE—you all have it already within yourselves. None was ever born without it. However you may deny it, it continually asserts itself. What is human love? It is more or less an affirmation of that unity: "I am one with thee, my wife, my child, my friend!"

— VIVEKANANDA

THE UNRELATED HUMAN being lacks wholeness, for he can achieve wholeness only through the soul, and the soul cannot exist without its other side, which is always found in a "You." Wholeness is a combination of I and You, and these show themselves to be parts of a transcendent unity whose nature can only be grasped symbolically, as in the symbols of the *rotundum,* the rose, the wheel or the *conjunctio Solis et Lunae* [the mystic marriage of sun and moon].

— CARL GUSTAV JUNG

ABOVE ALL, SEXUAL LOVE is the most intense and dramatic of the common ways in which a human being comes into union and conscious relationship with something outside himself. It is, furthermore, the most vivid of man's customary expressions of his organic spontaneity, the most positive and creative occasion of his being transported by something beyond his conscious will.

— ALAN WATTS

WHEN SEXUAL DESIRE IS also love it connects us with the whole world and becomes a new mode of experience. Sex then reveals itself as the great connective principle whereby we overcome duality, the force which made separateness as an aspect of oneness at some moment of bliss in the mind of God.

— IRIS MURDOCH

Eros is the drive toward union with what we belong to—union with our own possibilities, union with significant other persons in our world in relation to whom we discover our own self-fulfillment. Eros is the yearning in man which leads him to dedicate himself to seeking *arête,* the noble and good life.

— ROLLO MAY

TO LOVE IS TO DISCOVER
and complete one's self in someone other than oneself.

— PIERRE TEILHARD DE CHARDIN

W<small>HAT</small> <small>DOES</small> <small>ONE</small> <small>PER-</small>
son give to another? He gives of himself, of the most
precious he has, he gives of his life. This does not necessarily mean that he sacrifices his life for the other—but
that he gives him of that which is alive in him; he gives
him of his joy, of his interest, of his understanding, of
his knowledge, of his humor, of his sadness—of all expressions and manifestations of that which is alive in
him. In thus giving of his life, he enriches the other
person, he enhances the other's sense of aliveness by
enhancing his own sense of aliveness. He does not give
in order to receive; giving is in itself exquisite joy. But
in giving he cannot help bringing something to life in
the other person, and this which is brought to life reflects back to him; in truly giving, he cannot help receiving that which is given back to him. Giving implies to
make the other person a giver also and they both share
in the joy of what they have brought to life. In the act
of giving something is born, and both persons involved
are grateful for the life that is born for both of them.

— ERICH FROMM

Most of us would rather love than be loved. Almost everyone wants to be the lover. And the curt truth is that, in a deep secret way, the state of being beloved is intolerable to many. The beloved fears and hates the lover, and with the best of reasons. For the lover is for ever trying to strip bare his beloved. The lover craves any possible relation with the beloved, even if this experience can cause him only pain.

— CARSON McCULLERS

Yes, love, who showers benignity upon the world, and before whose presence all harsh passions flee and perish; the author of all soft affections; the destroyer of all ungentle thoughts; merciful, mild; the object of the admiration of the wise, and the delight of gods; possessed by the fortunate, and desired by the unhappy, therefore unhappy because they possess him not; the father of persuasion, and desire; the cherisher of all that is good, the abolisher of all evil; our most excellent pilot, defence, saviour and guardian in labour and in fear, in desire and in reason; the ornament and governor of all things human and divine; the best, the loveliest; in whose footsteps every one ought to follow, celebrating him excellently in song, and bearing each his part in that divinest harmony which Love sings to all things which live and are, soothing the troubled minds of gods and men.

— PLATO

FOR ONE HUMAN BEING to love another human being: that is perhaps the most difficult task that has been entrusted to us, the ultimate task, the final test and proof, the work for which all other work is merely preparation.

— RAINER MARIA RILKE

AND SO, TOO, I SPEAK OF love: he who is held by it is held by the strongest of bonds, and yet the stress is pleasant. Moreover, he can sweetly bear all that happens to him. When one has found this bond, he looks for no other.

— MEISTER ECKHART

Love does not consist in gazing at each other, but in looking outward in the same direction.

— ANTOINE DE SAINT-EXUPÉRY

You CAN'T WORSHIP LOVE and individuality in the same breath. Love is a mutual relationship, like a flame between wax and air. If either wax or air insists on getting its own way, or getting its own back too much, the flame goes out and the unison disappears. At the same time, if one yields itself up to the other entirely, there is a guttering mess. You have to balance love and individuality, and actually sacrifice a portion of each.

— D. H. LAWRENCE

LOVE IS THE PRODUCTIVE form of relatedness to others and to oneself. It implies responsibility, care, respect, and knowledge, and the wish for the other person to grow and develop. It is the expression of intimacy between two human beings under the condition of the preservation of each other's integrity.

— ERICH FROMM

A COMPLETE SHARING between two people is an impossibility, and whenever it seems, nevertheless, to exist, it is a narrowing, a mutual agreement which robs either one member or both of his fullest freedom and development. But, once the realization is accepted that, even between the closest human beings, infinite distances continue to exist, a wonderful living side by side can grow up, if they succeed in loving the distance between them which makes it possible for each to see the other whole and against a wide sky!

— RAINER MARIA RILKE

In contrast to symbiotic union, mature *love* is *union under the condition of preserving one's integrity,* one's individuality. *Love is an active power in man;* a power which breaks through the walls which separate man from his fellow men, which unites him with others; love makes him overcome the sense of isolation and separateness, yet it permits him to be himself, to retain his integrity. In love the paradox occurs that two beings become one and yet remain two.

— ERICH FROMM

Because passionate love breaks down walls and at first does it in such a sovereign way, we are rarely willing to admit how little that initial barrier-breaking is going to count when it comes to the slow, difficult, accepting of each other, when it comes to the irritations and abrasions, and the collisions, too, between two isolated human beings who want to be joined in a lasting relationship. So the walls go up again. The moment's vision is clouded, and mostly, I believe, by the fear of pain, our own and that of the other's by the fear of rejection. To be honest is to expose wounds, and also to wound. There is no preventing that. Union on a deep level is so costly that it very rarely takes place.

— MAY SARTON

I<small>N ORDER TO DEVELOP</small> love—universal love, cosmic love, whatever you would like to call it—one must accept the whole situation of life as it is, both the light and the dark, the good and the bad. One must open oneself to life, communicate with it.

— CHÖGYAM TRUNGPA

To LOVE MEANS TO OPEN ourselves to the negative as well as the positive—to grief, sorrow, and disappointment as well as to joy, fulfillment, and an intensity of consciousness we did not know was possible before.

— ROLLO MAY

To FEAR LOVE IS TO FEAR
life, and those who fear life are already three parts dead.

— BERTRAND RUSSELL

IN THE CO-EMERGENCE of love and fear we feel the paradox of being human in a most poignant way. It would be so much easier if we could just remain self-contained and establish an impeccable set of conditions to protect us from risk. Or if we could simply open to someone without question, let ourselves go, and completely lose ourselves in merging together. Yet both these alternatives undermine love, *for they destroy the tension between self and other, known and unknown, that love actually thrives on.*

— JOHN WELWOOD

To LOVE AT ALL IS TO BE vulnerable. Love anything, and your heart will certainly be wrung and possibly be broken. If you want to make sure of keeping it intact, you must give your heart to no one, not even to an animal. Wrap it carefully round with hobbies and little luxuries; avoid all entanglements; lock it up safe in the casket or coffin of your selfishness. But in that casket—safe, dark, motionless, airless—it will change. It will not be broken; it will become unbreakable, impenetrable, irredeemable. The alternative to tragedy, or at least to the risk of tragedy, is damnation. The only place outside Heaven where you can be perfectly safe from all the dangers and perturbations of love is Hell.

— C. S. LEWIS

OF ALL FORMS OF CAUTION, caution in love is perhaps the most fatal to true happiness.

— BERTRAND RUSSELL

LOVE UNFOLDS IN A human being traits of his which he never knew in himself. In love there is much both of the Stone Age and of the Witches' Sabbath. By anything less than love many men cannot be induced to commit a crime, to be guilty of a treason, to reanimate in themselves such feelings as they thought to have killed out long ago. In love is hidden an infinity of egoism, vanity, and selfishness. Love is the potent force that tears off all masks, and men who run away from love do so in order that they may preserve their masks.

— P. D. OUSPENSKY

WE BOTH STARTED OUT
with the desire to be devoted, complete, human, noble, faithful; but our passions broke the dam, and forced us into lies. We were never reconciled to our treacheries, to the impetuosity of our nature, to our evolutions and transitions, which made us humanly unreliable. As D. H. Lawrence said: "Every human being is treacherous to every other human being. Because he has to be true to his own soul."

But we dream of union, faithfulness.

— ANAÏS NIN

Since desire always goes towards that which is our direct opposite, it forces us to love that which will make us suffer.

— MARCEL PROUST

THE PEOPLE WE LOVE ARE built into us. Every day I am suddenly aware of something someone taught me long ago—or just yesterday—of some certainty and self-awareness that grew out of conflict with someone I loved enough to try to encompass, however painful that effort may have been.

— MAY SARTON

Love grows in depth
by virtue of the lovers experiencing encounter with each
other, conflict and growth, all over a period of time.
These cannot be omitted from any lasting and viable
experience of love. They involve choice and will under
whatever names you use.

— ROLLO MAY

GREAT LOVE—THE KIND that illumines and transforms us—always includes a keen awareness of limitation as well. Though love may inspire us to expand and develop in new ways, we can never be all things to the one we love, or someone other than who we are. Yet once accepted, limitation also helps us develop essential qualities, such as patience, determination, compassion, and humor. When love comes down to earth—bringing to light those dark corners we would prefer to ignore, encompassing all the different parts of who we are—it gains depth and power.

— JOHN WELWOOD

LOVE IS NOT A MERE impulse, it must contain truth, which is law. It accepts limitations from truth because of its own inner wealth. The child willingly exercises restraint to correct its bodily balance, because it has true pleasure in the freedom of its movements; and love also counts no cost as too great to realize its truth.

— RABINDRANATH TAGORE

LOVE CONSISTS IN THIS, that two solitudes protect, and touch, and greet each other.

— RAINER MARIA RILKE

"LONELINESS" FOR ME IS associated with love relationships. We are lonely when there is not perfect communion. In solitude one can achieve a good relationship with oneself. . . . I could never speak of "bone loneliness" now, though I have certainly experienced it when I was in love.

— MAY SARTON

PERHAPS A GREAT LOVE is never returned. Had it been given warmth and shelter by its counterpart in the Other, perhaps it would have been hindered from ever growing to maturity.

It "gives" us nothing. But in its world of loneliness it leads us up to summits with wide vistas—of insight.

— DAG HAMMARSKJÖLD

Where love reigns, there is no will to power; and where the will to power is paramount, love is lacking. The one is but the shadow of the other.

— CARL GUSTAV JUNG

A SOULFUL RELATION-
ship offers two difficult challenges: one, to come to
know oneself—the ancient oracle of Apollo; and two, to
get to know the deep, often subtle richness in the soul
of the other. Giving attention to one side usually helps
the other. As you get to know the other deeply, you will
discover much about yourself. Especially in moments of
conflict and maybe even despair, being open to the demands of a relationship can provide an extraordinary
opportunity for self-knowledge. It provides an occasion
to glimpse your own soul and notice its longings and its
fears. And as you get to know yourself, you can be more
accepting and understanding of the other's depth of
soul.

— THOMAS MOORE

PUT AWAY THE BOOK, the description, the tradition, the authority, and take the journey of self-discovery. Love, and don't be caught in opinions and ideas about what love is or should be. When you love, everything will come right. Love has its own action. Love, and you will know the blessings of it. Keep away from the authority who tells you what love is and what it is not. No authority knows and he who knows cannot tell. Love, and there is understanding.

— J. KRISHNAMURTI

THE ONLY WAY OF FULL knowledge lies in the *act* of love: this act transcends thought, it transcends words. It is the daring plunge into the experience of union. However, knowledge in thought, that is psychological knowledge, is a necessary condition for full knowledge in the act of love. I have to know the other person and myself objectively, in order to be able to see his reality, or rather, to overcome the illusions, the irrationally distorted picture I have of him. Only if I know a human being objectively, can I know him in his ultimate essence, in the act of love.

— ERICH FROMM

We really have to understand the person we want to love. If our love is only a will to possess, it is not love. If we only think of ourselves, if we know only our own needs and ignore the needs of the other person, we cannot love. We must look deeply in order to see and understand the needs, aspirations, and suffering of the person we love. This is the ground of real love. You cannot resist loving another person when you really understand him or her.

— THICH NHAT HANH

"I TAUGHT HIM," HE quavered, "to trust in love. I said: "When love comes, that is reality." I said: "Passion does not blind. No. Passion is sanity, and the woman you love, she is the only person you will ever really understand."

— E. M. FORSTER

ONE ALWAYS LOVES
the person who understands you.

— ANAÏS NIN

THE SOURCE OF LOVE IS deep in us, and we can help others realize a lot of happiness. One word, one action, or one thought can reduce another person's suffering and bring him joy. One word can give comfort and confidence, destroy doubt, help someone avoid a mistake, reconcile a conflict, or open the door to liberation. One action can save a person's life or help him take advantage of a rare opportunity. One thought can do the same, because thoughts always lead to words and actions. If love is in our heart, every thought, word, and deed can bring about a miracle. Because understanding is the very foundation of love, words and actions that emerge from our love are always helpful.

— THICH NHAT HANH

PRACTICE OF SACRED RE-lationship is practice of good relation with all in the family of life. Thus the Pale One gave seven reminders to the people, that all might recall and honor the unity of the hoop. . . . Arising from these teachings are the nine precepts in the Code of Right Relationship: 1. Speak only words of truth. 2. Speak only of the good qualities of others. 3. Be a confidant and carry no tales. 4. Turn aside the veil of anger to release the beauty inherent in all. 5. Waste not the bounty, and want not. 6. Honor the light in all. Compare nothing; see all for its suchness. 7. Respect all life; cut away ignorance from one's own heart. 8. Neither kill nor harbor thoughts of angry nature, which destroy peace like an arrow. 9. Do it now; if you see what needs doing, do it.

— DHYANI YWAHOO

A GOOD RELATIONSHIP has a pattern like a dance and is built on some of the same rules. The partners do not need to hold on tightly, because they move confidently in the same pattern, intricate but gay and swift and free, like a country dance of Mozart's. To touch heavily would be to arrest the pattern and freeze the movement, to check the endlessly changing beauty of its unfolding. There is no place here for the possessive clutch, the clinging arm, the heavy hand; only the barest touch in passing. Now arm in arm, now face to face, now back to back—it does not matter which. Because they know they are partners moving to the same rhythm, creating a pattern together, and being invisibly nourished by it.

The joy of such a pattern is not only the joy of creation or the joy of participation, it is also the joy of living in the moment. Lightness of touch and living in the moment are intertwined. One cannot dance well unless one is completely in time with the music, not leaning back to the last step or pressing forward to the next one, but poised directly on the present step as it comes. Perfect poise on the beat is what gives good dancing its sense of ease, of timelessness, of the eternal.

— ANNE MORROW LINDBERGH

How to convey the
rapture of the mind, as it mingles with the body, draws
apart into itself, and mingles again, in a wild and yet
graceful dance? The sense of being absolutely in the
right and longed-for place is fixed and guaranteed by
every ray in the universe. . . . Consciousness half swoons
with its sense of humble delighted privilege while keen
sight, in between the explosions of the stars, devours
every detail of the real presence. I am here now, you are
here now, we are here now. . . . There is also a gleeful
calm as one realizes that these passing seconds are the
fullest and most perfect, not even excluding sexual
union, which can be allotted to human beings.

— IRIS MURDOCH

Have we actually a relationship with another? To be related means to be in contact. You may be sexually, physically in contact but that does not constitute a relationship. We are talking of a relationship in which there is no image between you and another. I do not know if you have ever tried it. Do. Have no image about your wife, your husband, your neighbour, or about another; just look, just see, directly, without the image, the symbol, the memory of yesterday, of what she said to you, what you said to her, how she annoyed you and all the rest of it. Stripped of these things there is a possibility of right relationship. Because then everything in that relationship is new; relationship is no longer of the dead past.

— J. KRISHNAMURTI

LOVE CAN BE FULFILLED without becoming trapped in the web of emotional needs. We can learn from the virtue of a well which exists for all to take from. Its spring never runs dry. When our inner treasure is inexhaustible, we can provide limitless love and still remain independent and non-possessing.

In our tradition, we can enjoy the sunrise within us every moment. Our love is as free as the blowing wind and as enduring as a flowing river. Since we continually renew ourselves, we do not fear losing love. Our cultivation becomes our lover, for our love is Tao. Thus, love never withers, for it is continually refreshed.

— HUA-CHING NI

Relationship, as I understand it, has to do with the exquisitely tuned harmonics between two people who are attempting to become conscious of their personal psychology. The mystery of each individual is holy, and the mystery which brings each into relationship with the other is tenuous, invisible, and sacred. As Jung wrote when his friend Father Victor White died, "The living mystery of life is always hidden between Two, and it is the true mystery which cannot be betrayed by words and depleted by arguments."

In such a relationship, both partners are attempting to become more conscious of their complexes and their masculine and feminine sides, both are willing to reflect on their interaction, and both have the courage to honor the uniqueness of what they share. Neither is attempting to possess the other, neither wishes to be possessed. The relationship itself is unburdened by the pressure of inchoate needs and expectations. The partners do not demand a "whole" relationship, nor do they seek to be made whole by it; rather they value the relationship as a container in which is reflected the wholeness they seek in themselves. Each is free to be authentic. Living in the *now,* unfettered by collective ideas of how either should act or be, they have no way of knowing how such a relationship will develop. If they persevere, they may experience the grace of the unicorn.

— MARION WOODMAN

BE COURAGEOUS IN giving and receiving love. Love is a stream and we are all part of it. We can be fished from the sea of ignorance in an instant; the line is right above our heads and can always be grasped with our hands. It is for us to lift from our attachment to ignorance, pain, and desire to recognition of the moment. It is not to deny what is in the process of correction. It is to acknowledge the good and to be in the moment, to see each moment for its wholeness and to appreciate it as a unique gift. That is a discipline in itself: to be still, to be loving, to know "I am in this moment creating cause for all moments."

— DHYANI YWAHOO

SEX IS SAVED FROM SELF-destruction by eros, and this is the normal condition. But eros cannot live without philia, brotherly love and friendship. The tension of continuous attraction and continuous passion would be unbearable if it lasted forever. Philia is the relaxation in the presence of the beloved which accepts the other's being as being; it is simply liking to be with the other, liking to rest with the other, liking the rhythm of the walk, the voice, the whole being of the other. This gives a width to eros; it gives it time to grow; time to sink its roots down deeper. Philia does not require that we do anything for the beloved except accept him, be with him, and enjoy him. It is friendship in the simplest, most direct terms.

— ROLLO MAY

WHEN TWO PEOPLE ARE "in love," people commonly say that they are "more than just friends." But in the long run, they seem to treat each other as *less* than friends. Most people think that being "in love" is a much more intimate, much more "meaningful," relationship than "mere" friendship. Why, then, do couples refuse each other the selfless love, the kindness and good will, that they readily give to their friends? People can't ask of their friends that they carry all their projections, be scapegoats for all their moods, keep them feeling happy, and make life complete for them. Why do couples impose these demands on each other? Because the cult of romance teaches us that we have the right to expect that all our projections will be borne—all our desires satisfied, and all our fantasies made to come true—in the person we are "in love" with. In one of the Hindu rites of marriage, the bride and groom make to each other a solemn statement: "You will be my *best friend.*" Western couples need to learn to be friends, to live with each other in a spirit of friendship, to take the quality of friendship as a guide through the tangles we have made of love.

— ROBERT JOHNSON

INFANTILE LOVE FOLLOWS the principle: *"I love because I am loved."* Mature love follows the principle: *"I am loved because I love."* Immature love says: *"I love you because I need you."* Mature love says: *"I need you because I love you."*

— ERICH FROMM

MATURITY INVOLVES LEARNING to create relationships in which there are both excitement and comfort, sex and caring, spontaneity and continuity. But relational maturity doesn't just happen. It is an art and a significant achievement to create an erotic friendship. And it doesn't usually happen when we are in our teens or early twenties. For good reason. In our teens and twenties we need to explore different types of relationships to discover what is and is not satisfying. Puppy love and early romances teach us that pure romance lasts about ninety days and is not a good basis for a lasting relationship.

— SAM KEEN

Hᴏᴡ ᴜɴɴᴀᴛᴜʀᴀʟ ᴛʜᴇ imposed view, imposed by a puritanical ethos, that passionate love belongs only to the young, that people are dead from the neck down by the time they are forty, and that any deep feeling, any passion after that age, is either ludicrous or revolting. The French have always known that our capacity for loving mellows and ripens, and love if it is any good at all gets better with age. Perhaps it is not the puritan in us who has spread this myth. Perhaps it is just the opposite; the revolt against puritanism has opened up a new ethos where sex is the god, and thus the sexual athlete is the true hero. Here the middle-aged or old are at a disadvantage. Where we have the advantage is in loving itself—we know so much more; we are so much better able to handle anxiety, frustration, or even our own romanticism; and deep down we have such a store of tenderness.

— MAY SARTON

THE CONFRONTATION WITH death—and the reprieve from it—makes everything look so precious, so sacred, so beautiful that I feel more strongly than ever the impulse to love it, to embrace it, and to let myself be overwhelmed by it. My river has never looked so beautiful. . . . Death, and its ever present possibility, makes love, passionate love, more possible. I wonder if we could love passionately, if ecstasy would be possible at all, if we knew we'd never die.

— ABRAHAM MASLOW

TAKE HOLD TIGHTLY; LET go lightly. This is one of the great secrets of felicity in love.

— A. R. ORAGE

INTERESTINGLY, WE SAY "falling" in love, and not "rising" into love. Love is an act of surrender to another person; it is total abandonment. In love you give yourself over, you let go, and you say, "I give myself to you." To many people this seems quite mad because it means letting things get out of control, and all sensible people keep things in control. Actually, the course of wisdom, what is really sensible, is to let go, to commit oneself, to give oneself up; and this is considered quite mad. It is thus that we are driven to the strange conclusion that in madness lies sanity.

— ALAN WATTS

THERE WERE THOSE BRIEF meetings . . . which were of an intensity that, for me at least, was greater than anything before. It was all thanks to that lack of attachment; all my love and sympathy and concern and happiness went out to him, but I made no more demands on him, I wanted nothing from him, I took him as he was and enjoyed him.

— ETTY HILLESUM

WE WANT TO BE SURE OF love, to peg it down, so that it won't elude us; we reach conclusions, make agreements about it; we call it by various names, with their special meanings; we talk about "my love," just as we talk about "my property," "my family," "my virtue," and we hope to lock it safely away, so that we can turn to other things and make sure of them too; but somehow it's always slipping away when we least expect it.

— J. KRISHNAMURTI

Security in a relationship lies neither in looking back to what it was in nostalgia, nor forward to what it might be in dread or anticipation, but living in the present relationship and accepting it as it is now. For relationships, too, must be like islands. One must accept them for what they are here and now, within their limits—islands, surrounded and interrupted by the sea, continually visited and abandoned by the tides. One must accept the security of the winged life, of ebb and flow, of intermittency.

— ANNE MORROW LINDBERGH

Our love becomes impoverished if we lack the courage to sacrifice its object.

— DAG HAMMARSKJÖLD

It seems to me the most important thing in surrendering a close bond is sacrificing the relationship without sacrificing the love. If life is an "opening out like the rose that can no longer keep closed," then everything we love is an opening of a petal. When the thorns are accepted love abides. The profound relationships in our lives, whatever their outcome, have given us the riches of loving and that wealth is the only wealth that means anything in the end.

— MARION WOODMAN

WE OFTEN ASSUME THAT once two people have come together, they should never part; yet relationships are always ending, and people drift apart as naturally as they turn toward new connections. I'm not suggesting that we should simply be realistic and acknowledge the bitter truth that relationships end; the sense that they will go on forever is always a part of making new connections. But when they do end, we may have to face the dark and demanding will of the gods, which often goes against all human desire. We can take that lesson home and lodge it in our hearts—life is a constant interchange between human will and divine providence. We need both the courage to plan and create a life, and piety of the most profound kind in relation to the mysteries that undergird it.

— THOMAS MOORE

THE IDEA OF RELATION-
ship needs to fall apart. When we realize that life is the
expression of death and death is the expression of life,
that continuity cannot exist without discontinuity, then
there is no longer any need to cling to one and fear the
other. There is no longer any ground for the brave or
the cowardly. One sees that relationship is the lack of
any viewpoint whatsoever.

— CHÖGYAM TRUNGPA

So LONG AS WE ARE
concretizing, love is lost. We are trying to make something happen our way to satisfy our own ego desires. If,
for example, I invite you to my home for dinner, hoping
to impress you with my Chippendale furniture, my suc-
culent chicken Kiev, my perfectly landscaped garden,
then I am concretizing my Self. My ideal of perfection
is projected; in effect, I identify with God when I believe
I am in control in my little kingdom. If, on the other
hand, I am in my own Being, then I invite you to my
home because I love you and choose to share these
beautiful objects that I love with you. They are a manifestation of my inner Reality, but my Reality is not projected into them. When the ego is conscious enough to
recognize the Self—the kingdom of God within—it
does not project the perfection outside. It is the dead
god that is projected into the concretized perfection; the
ego, caught in a massive inflation, is denying the inner
Reality. Happening cannot happen. So long as we project onto the collective world—institutions, media, society—an authority it does not rightfully possess, we are
allowing ourselves to be contaminated by alien elements.
If we allow the Self to come to consciousness, the au-

thority is inside. Happening happens. We make the space, we unlock the door, and wait. We surrender to ravishment.

— MARION WOODMAN

Sunlight pours into my study from four windows. Year by year the turquoise silk has faded to a gentle watery blue, the brilliant embroidery has softened, and it is lovelier than ever. "We love the things we love for what they are," Robert Frost reminds us. And he means, I think, that we love them as they change—he is speaking in the poem of a brook gone dry—as well as for what they once were.

— MAY SARTON

ONE LEARNS TO ACCEPT the fact that no permanent return is possible to an old form of relationship; and, more deeply still, that there is no holding of a relationship to a single form. This is not tragedy but part of the ever-recurrent miracle of life and growth. All living relationships are in process of change, of expansion, and must perpetually be building themselves new forms. But there is no single fixed form to express such a changing relationship.

— ANNE MORROW LINDBERGH

I POURED OUT ALL MY tenderness, all the tenderness one cannot express for a man even when one loves him very, very much. I poured it all out into the great, all-embracing spring night. I stood on the little bridge and looked across the water; I melted into the landscape and offered all my tenderness up to the sky and the stars and the water and to the little bridge. And that was the best moment of the day.

And I felt this was the only way of transforming all the many and deep and tender feelings one carries for another into deeds: to entrust them to nature, to let them stream out under the open spring sky and to realise that there is no other way of letting them go.

— ETTY HILLESUM

I THINK THERE'S A DI-
mension of love that's far beyond what we yet know in
terms of healing, in terms of expansion. You can experience the healing that's going on through the love that
exists between two people; you can see the light in the
other's body and you can feel it in your own. It's a huge
energy.

— MARION WOODMAN

Love comforteth
like sunshine after rain.

— WILLIAM SHAKESPEARE

IF I ANSWER THE APPEAL to become a lover, it is no nebulous or general essence of mankind I am called to love, but my self, my children, my wife, my friends, my community, my land, my people, my tools, my world. The lover heals the world not by a vague and abstract love for everybody and everything, but by becoming passionate and vowing fidelity to concrete relationships, persons, institutions, and places. The only *Beyond* I can know is the one found *within* the intimate experience of the world as it is given to me.

— SAM KEEN

THE ESSENTIAL LOVE TO which we refer, that experience of pure being, heals the chasm of the personal and separate. It is the love that goes beyond "love," beyond conditions, which finishes our business. For to finish our business means an end of relationships as business; it is not a totaling of accounts, not a trade-off of you "understanding me" and me "acknowledging you," but instead a letting go of that other person as separate and touching him or her with forgiveness and mercy. No longer involved in the commerce of relationships so much as committed to the process of relating. To finish business with others allows us to come to completion with ourselves, the first step and the last on the path of healing.

— STEPHEN LEVINE

To love is to be about the task of healing. The lover's vocation is to lure others (and that part of the self that nurses old injuries and fears, takes pride in autonomy, and harbors the illusion of self-sufficiency) into re-cognition of their true being and their true allegiance. It is to practice the art of forgiveness and to expand the circle of care. Love's way is always vulnerable because it abandons the rules of power-politics and the paranoid game upon which the social consensus is based.

In the passionate life, one is always in the process of forgetting one's self and becoming self-transcending spirit. The lover hovers on the edge of disappearing in empathy. In compassion we live on the boundary, a no-man's land. At any moment we may forget the self and slip into a wood thrush's song, the cry of an injured old man, or a lover's arms. In love, the moth becomes the flame. In compassion, we burn and bond with the other.

To love is to return to a home we never left, to remember who we are.

— SAM KEEN

THE FOREVERNESS OF REAL love is one of the reasons why even unrequited love is a source of joy. The human soul craves for the eternal of which, apart from certain rare mysteries of religion, only love and art can give a glimpse. . . . Love brings with it also a vision of selflessness. How right Plato was to think that, embracing a lovely boy, he was on the road to the Good. I say a *vision* of selflessness, because our mixed nature readily degrades the purity of any aspiration. But such insight, even intermittent, even momentary, is a privilege and can be of permanent value because of the intensity with which it visits us. Ah, even once, to *will* another rather than oneself! Why could we not make of this revelation a lever by which to lift the world? Why cannot this release from self provide a foothold in a new place which we can then colonize and enlarge until at last we will *all* that is not ourselves? That was Plato's dream. It is not impossible.

— IRIS MURDOCH

FREE PASSION IS RADIATION without a radiator, a fluid, pervasive warmth that flows effortlessly. It is not destructive because it is a balanced state of being and highly intelligent. By opening, by dropping our self-conscious grasping, we see not only the surface of an object, but we see the whole way through. We appreciate not in terms of sensational qualities alone, but we see in terms of whole qualities, which are pure gold. We are not overwhelmed by the exterior, but seeing the exterior simultaneously puts us through to the interior. So we reach the heart of the situation and, if this is a meeting of two people, the relationship is very inspiring because we do not see the other person purely in terms of physical attraction or habitual patterns. We see the inside as well as the outside.

— CHÖGYAM TRUNGPA

AT WHAT MOMENT DO lovers come into the most complete possession of *themselves,* if not when they are *lost* in each other?

— PIERRE TEILHARD DE CHARDIN

It had been a cool day and the sky had been open and there was the light of a thousand winters; it was short, penetrating and expansive; it went with you everywhere, it wouldn't leave you. Like perfume, it was in the most unexpected places; it seemed to have entered into the most secret corners of one's being. It was a light that left no shadow and every shadow lost its depth; because of it, all substance lost its density; it was as though you looked through everything, through the trees on the other side of the wall, through your own self. Your self was as opaque as the sky and as open. It was intense and to be with it was to be passionate, not the passion of feeling or desire, but a passion that would never wither or die. It was a strange light, it exposed everything and made it vulnerable, and what had no protection was love. You couldn't be what you were, you were burnt out, without leaving any ashes and unexpectedly there was not a thing but that light.

— J. KRISHNAMURTI

THE MIND OF LOVE brings peace, joy, and happiness to ourselves and others. Mindful observation is the element which nourishes the tree of understanding, and compassion and love are the most beautiful flowers. When we realize the mind of love, we have to go to the one who has been the object of our mindful observation, so that our mind of love is not just an object of our imagination, but a source of energy which has a real effect in the world.

— THICH NHAT HANH

Love is an extraordinary thing; without it, life is barren. You may have many possessions and sit in the seat of power, but without the beauty and greatness of love, life soon becomes misery and confusion. Love implies . . . that those who are loved be left wholly free to grow in their fullness, to be something greater than mere social machines. Love does not compel, either openly or through the subtle threat of duties and responsibilities. Where there's any form of compulsion or exertion of authority, there's no love.

— J. KRISHNAMURTI

Beside our need for a meaning, also a need for human intimacy without conventional trappings—for the experience of a circle where power expresses itself in meaningful and beautiful forms. The holiness of human life, before which we bow down in worship.

— DAG HAMMARSKJÖLD

WHEN THE TIME COMES that you feel love for someone, be gentle. Love has a delicate nature. Never be rough with it or it will be completely destroyed. Always distinguish the difference between love and desire. Love gives pleasure; desire creates pressure. Desire, loneliness, tension and disappointment can all deteriorate the delicate nature of true love. To love is to be gentle. Tender love is truly beneficial in any circumstance. If love is not given gently, it becomes stormy. Stormy love, like stormy weather, can never last long.

— HUA-CHING NI

It isn't possible to love and to part. You will wish that it was. You can transmute love, ignore it, muddle it, but you can never pull it out of you. I know by experience that the poets are right: love is eternal.

— E. M. FORSTER

WHAT IS MOST ADMIRABLE in Love is, that he neither inflicts nor endures injury in his relations either with Gods or men. Nor if he suffers any thing does he suffer it through violence, nor doing any thing does he act it with violence, for Love is never even touched with violence. Every one willingly administers every thing to Love; and that which every one voluntarily concedes to another, the laws, which are the kings of the republic, decree that is just for him to possess. In addition to justice, Love participates in the highest temperance; for if temperance is defined to be the being superior to and holding under dominion pleasures and desires; then Love, than whom no pleasure is more powerful, and who is thus more powerful than all persuasions and delights, must be excellently temperate. In power and valour Mars cannot contend with Love: the love of Venus possesses Mars; the possessor is always superior to the possessed, and he who subdues the most powerful must of necessity be the most powerful of all.

— PLATO

Love conquers
all things: let us too give in to Love.

— VIRGIL

I MAY SPEAK IN TONGUES of men or of angels, but if I am without love, I am a sounding gong or a clanging cymbal. I may have the gift of prophecy, and know every hidden truth; I may have faith strong enough to move mountains; but if I have no love, I am nothing. I may dole out all I possess, or even give my body to be burnt, but if I have no love, I am none the better.

Love is patient; love is kind and envies no one. Love is never boastful, nor conceited, nor rude; never selfish, not quick to take offence. Love keeps no score of wrongs; does not gloat over other men's sins, but delights in the truth. There is nothing love cannot face; there is no limit to its faith, its hope, and its endurance.

Love will never come to an end. Are there prophets? their work will be over. Are their tongues of ecstasy? they will cease. Is there knowledge? it will vanish away; for our knowledge and our prophecy alike are partial, and the partial vanishes when wholeness comes. When I was a child, my speech, my outlook, and my thoughts were all childish. When I grew up, I had finished with childish things. Now we see only puzzling reflections in a mirror, but then we shall see face to face. My knowledge now is partial; then it will be whole, like God's knowledge of me. In a word, there are three things that last for ever: faith, hope, and love; but the greatest of them all is love.

— SAINT PAUL

LOVE—
stronger than Death and harder than Hell.

— MEISTER ECKHART

LOVE WALKS NOT UPON the earth, nor over the heads of men, which are not indeed very soft; but he dwells within, and treads on the softest of existing things, having established his habitation within the souls and inmost nature of gods and men; not indeed in all souls—for wherever he chances to find a hard and rugged disposition, there he will not inhabit, but only where it is most soft and tender. Of needs must he be the most delicate of all things, who touches lightly with his feet only the softest parts of those things which are the softest of all.

— PLATO

WITH EVERY OCCURRENCE in life and its contrasting situations that relates to love, it is best to make no attempt to understand, since in so far as these are as inexorable as they are unlooked-for, they appear to be governed by magic rather than by rational laws.

— MARCEL PROUST

Relationship is not only about the people who interact with each other. It is a vehicle as well to the absolute factors that shape human life fundamentally. Every relationship that touches the soul leads us into a dialogue with eternity, so that, even though we may think our strong emotions focus on the people around us, we are being set face to face with divinity itself, however we understand or speak that mystery.

— THOMAS MOORE

THE HEIGHT OF SEXUAL love, coming upon us of itself, is one of the most total experiences of relationship to the other of which we are capable, but prejudice and insensitivity have prevented us from seeing that in any other circumstances such delight would be called mystical ecstasy. For what lovers feel for each other in this moment is no other than adoration in its full religious sense, and its climax is almost literally the pouring of their lives into each other. Such adoration, which is due only to God, would indeed be idolatrous were it not that in that moment love takes away illusion and shows the beloved for what he or she in truth is—not the socially pretended person but the naturally divine.

— ALAN WATTS

To LOVE COMPLETELY carries with it the threat of the annihilation of everything. This intensity of consciousness has something in common with the ecstasy of the mystic in his union with God: just as he can never be *sure* God is there, so love carries us to that intensity of consciousness in which we no longer have any guarantee of security.

— ROLLO MAY

LOVERS IN THEIR PLAY—
when they have been liberated from the traditions which bound them to the trivial or the gross conception of play in love—are thus moving amongst the highest human activities, alike of the body and of the soul. They are passing to each other the sacramental chalice of that wine which imparts the deepest joy that men and women can know. They are subtly weaving the invisible cords that bind husband and wife together more truly and more firmly than the priest of any church. And if in the end—as may or may not be—they attain the climax of free and complete union, then their human play has become one with that divine play of creation in which old poets fabled that, out of the dust of the ground and in his own image, some God of Chaos once created Man.

— HAVELOCK ELLIS

Is it only when you are in love with another person that you see them as they really are? In the ordinary way, when you are not in love with a person, could it be that you see only a fragmented version of that being? When you are in love with someone, you do indeed see them as a divine being. Now, suppose that is what they truly are and that your eyes have by your beloved been opened, in which case your beloved is serving to you as a kind of guru. This is the reason why there is a form of sexual yoga which is based upon the idea that man and woman are to each other as a mutual guru and student. Through a tremendous outpouring of psychic energy in total devotion and worship for this older person, who is respectively god or goddess, you realize, by total fusion and contact, the divine center in them. At once it bounces back to you and you discover your own.

— ALAN WATTS

As by an electric current that gives us a shock, I have been shaken by my loves, I have lived them, I have felt them: never have I succeeded in seeing or thinking them. Indeed I am inclined to believe that in these relationships (I leave out of account the physical pleasure which is their habitual accompaniment but is not enough in itself to constitute them), beneath the outward appearance of the woman, it is to those invisible forces with which she is incidentally accompanied that we address ourselves as to obscure deities. It is they whose good will is necessary to us, with whom we seek to establish contact without finding any positive pleasure in it. The woman herself, during our assignation with her, does little more than put us in touch with these goddesses.

— MARCEL PROUST

LOVE IN RELATION TO our life is a deity, sometimes terrible, sometimes benevolent, but never subservient to us, never consenting to serve our purposes. Men strive to subordinate love to themselves, to warp it to the uses of their every-day mode of life, and to their souls' uses; but it is impossible to subordinate love to anything, and it mercilessly revenges itself upon those little mortals who would subordinate *God* to themselves and make Him serve them. It confuses all their calculations, and forces them to do things which confound themselves, forcing them to serve *itself,* to do what *it* wants.

— P. D. OUSPENSKY

LOVE INTERPRETS AND
makes a communciation between divine and human
things, conveying the prayers and sacrifices of men to
the gods, and communicating the commands and directions concerning the mode of worship most pleasing to
them, from gods to men. He fills up that intermediate
space between these two classes of beings, so as to bind
together, by his own power, the whole universe of
things.

— PLATO

THE YOU ENCOUNTERS me by grace—it cannot be found by seeking. But that I speak the basic word to it is a deed of my whole being, is my essential deed.

The You encounters me. But I enter into a direct relationship to it. Thus the relationship is election and electing, passive and active at once: An action of the whole being must approach passivity, for it does away with all partial actions and thus with any sense of action, which always depends on limited exertions.

The basic word I-You can be spoken only with one's whole being. The concentration and fusion into a whole being can never be accomplished by me, can never be accomplished without me. I require a You to become; becoming I, I say You.

All actual life is encounter.

— MARTIN BUBER

KNOW THAT ALL OF OUR relationships are aspects of mind and that our thoughts are always contributing to the forms around us. Within every being there is the seed of our family's full unity; the opening of that great flower of the heart's wisdom is a moment of capitulation into the vastness of mind. When we affirm love and forgiveness as a stream within our hearts, we release in our bodies a great energy, and the sacred flow within us flows more readily, more fully. In that stream of forgiveness we see that we continue on in a process and that we have choice. Our words, our actions, our very breath shape the fiber of our reality. The rocks in the stream are part of the dream.

— DHYANI YWAHOO

So it is with life, and especially with love. There is no point. There is nothing you can cut out, except falsity, which isn't love or life. But the love itself is a flow, two little streams of feeling, one from the woman, one from the man, that flow and flow and never stop, and sometimes they twinkle with stars, sometimes they chafe, but still they flow on, intermingling; and if they rise to a floweriness like a daisy, that is part of the flow; and they will inevitably die down again, which is also part of a flow. And one relationship may produce many flowerinesses, as a daisy plant produces many daisies; but they will all die down again as the summer passes, though the green plant itself need not die. If flowers didn't fade they wouldn't be flowers, they'd be artificial things. But there are roots to faded flowers and in the root the flow continues and continues. And only the flow matters; live and let live, love and let love. There is no point to love.

— D. H. LAWRENCE

LOVE IS THE LAST ELE-
ment of form which takes us to the formless, a quality
of the mind which reflects the nature of the heart and
is the essential connection between the two. When love
fills the mind, it opens into the heart. It is a key to
reopen the connection whose experience is a sense of
fulfillment and wholeness. When a merciful awareness
is sent into mental or physical discomfort, the context
changes. Acceptance receives the moment like water,
yielding, absorbing.

— STEPHEN LEVINE

ONLY CONNECT! . . .
Only connect the prose and the passion, and both will
be exalted, and human love will be seen at its height.

— E. M. FORSTER

LOVE IS LIFE. ALL, EVERY-
thing that I understand, I understand only because I
love. Everything is, everything exists, only because I love.
Everything is united by it alone. Love is God, and to die
means that I, a particle of love, shall return to the general and eternal source.

— LEO TOLSTOY

deepdown torrent O and the sea the sea crimson sometimes like fire and the glorious sunsets and the figtrees in
the Alameda gardens yes and all the queer little streets and
pink and blue and yellow houses and the rosegardens and
the jessamine and geraniums and cactuses and Gibraltar as
a girl where I was a Flower of the mountain yes when I
put the rose in my hair like the Andalusian girls used or
shall I wear a red yes and how he kissed me under the
Moorish wall and I thought well as well him as another
and then I asked him with my eyes to ask again yes and
then he asked me would I yes to say yes my mountain
flower and first I put my arms around him yes and drew
him down to me so he could feel my breasts all perfume
yes and his heart was going like mad and yes I said yes I
will Yes.

— JAMES JOYCE

NOTES ON
THE CONTRIBUTORS
AND SOURCES

W. H. AUDEN (1907–1973) was a British-born American poet and essayist. "Belief in the . . ." (p. 8), "To love our neighbor . . ." (p. 33), from *A Certain World* (New York: Viking Press, 1970).

MARTIN BUBER (1878–1965), Austrian-born Jewish theologian and philospher, is best known for his book *I and Thou,* which concerns the relationship between God and the individual. "Every true deed is . . ." (p. 32), "The You encounters me . . ." (p. 136) from *I and Thou,* trans. Walter Kaufmann (New York: Charles Scribner's Sons, 1970).

FYODOR DOSTOEVSKY (1821–1881) was a pre-eminent Russian novelist whose works reflect his fascination with good and evil, suffering and redemption. "You are working . . ." (p. 37) from *The Brothers Karamazov,* trans. Constance Garnett (New York: Random House, 1977).

MEISTER ECKHART (c. 1260–1327) was a Dominican preacher and scholar of Strasbourg and Cologne whose popular and influential writings on mystical theology and philosophy were the first of their kind to appear in the German language. "If you love yourself . . ." (p. 34), "And so, too, . . ." (p. 48), "Love . . ." (p. 125) from *Meister Eckhart: A Modern Translation,* trans. Raymond B. Blakeney (New York: Harper & Row, 1941).

HAVELOCK ELLIS (1859–1939) was an English physician who compiled the first study of human sexuality from a detached perspective unmarred by guilt feelings. "Lovers in their play . . ." (p. 131) from *Little Essays of Love and Virtue* (London: A. & C. Black, 1922).

RALPH WALDO EMERSON (1803–1882), the American essayist, orator, and poet, was a bold advocate of spiritual independence and individualism. "He who is in love . . ." (p. 27) from "The Method of Nature" (oration, 1841).

E. M. FORSTER (1879–1970), English novelist and critic, is best known for his examination of British middle-class values and moral conflicts. " 'I taught him . . .' " (p. 76), "It isn't possible . . ." (p. 120), from *A Room with a View* (London: Edward Arnold, 1977); "Only connect! . . ." (p. 140) from *Howard's End* (New York: Bantam Books, 1985).

ERICH FROMM (1900–1980) was a German-born American psychoanalyst and social philosopher whose works emphasized in value of loving relationships in an impersonal industrialized society. "There is hardly any word . . ." (p. 13) from *Man for Himself: An Inquiry into the Psychology of Ethics* (New York: Holt, Rhinehart & Winston, 1947); "Love for man . . ." (p. 36) *Man for Himself;* "What does one person . . ." (p. 44) from *The Art of Loving* (New York: Harper & Row, 1989); "Love is the productive . . ." (p. 51) from *Man for Himself;* "In contrast . . ." (p. 53), "The only way . . ." (p. 74), "Infantile love . . ." (p. 89) from *The Art of Loving.*

DAG HAMMARSKJÖLD (1905–1961) was a Swedish statesman and secretary general of the United Nations from 1953 until his death in an air crash. He was awarded the Nobel peace prize after his death for his work as "the curator of the secrets of eighty-two nations." "Perhaps a great love . . ." (p. 70), "Our love becomes . . ."

(p. 98), "Beside our need . . ." (p. 118) from *Markings* (New York: Knopf, 1964).

THICH NHAT HANH is a Vietnamese-born Buddhist monk whose teachings are internationally renowned. "We really have to understand . . ." (p. 75), "The source of love . . ." (p. 78), "The mind of love . . ." (p. 116) from *Peace Is Every Step: The Path of Mindfulness in Everyday Life* (New York: Bantam Books, 1991).

HILDEGARD OF BINGEN (1098–1179), a Rhineland mystic, was a poet and scientist, painter and musician, healer and abbess, playwright, prophet, preacher, and social critic. "The young woman . . ." (p. 18) from *Book of Divine Works with Letters and Songs,* trans. Matthew Fox (Sante Fe, N.M.: Bear & Co., 1987).

ETTY HILLESUM (1914–1943) was born into a family of privileged and highly assimilated Dutch Jews. Her journals record the years 1941–1943 in Amsterdam, breaking off on her deportation to Auschwitz, where she died. "My heart will always fly . . ." (p. 24), "There were those brief meetings . . ." (p. 95), "I poured out . . ." (p. 106) from *An Interrupted Life* (New York: Pantheon Books, 1983).

ROBERT A. JOHNSON is a noted American author, lecturer, and Jungian analyst who has also studied at the Sri Aurobindo Ashram in India. "When two people . . ." (p. 88) from *We: Understanding the Psychology of Romantic Love* (New York: HarperCollins, 1983).

JAMES JOYCE (1892–1941), the great Irish writer, wrote short stories and novels renowned for their word play, comedy, and power of invention. "And O that awful deepdown . . ." (p. 142) from *Ulysses* (New York: Random House, 1992).

C. G. JUNG (1875–1961) was a Swiss psychiatrist who, after collaborating with and breaking from Sigmund Freud, went on to develop his own school of analytical psychology. "I have again and again . . ." (p. 10) from *Memories, Dreams, Reflections* (New York: Pantheon Books, 1962). "The unrelated human being . . ." (p. 39) from *The Psychology of the Transference* (Princeton, N.J.: Princeton University Press, 1969); "Where love reigns . . ." (p. 71) from *Psychological Reflections: A New Anthology of His Writings 1905–1961,* ed. Jolande Jaffe and R.F.C. Hull (Princeton, N.J.: Princeton University Press, 1970).

TOYOHIKO KAGAWA (1888–1960), a Japanese social reformer and evangelist, was a convert to Christianity. "Love is creation . . ." (p. 17) from *Love: The Law of Life* (Philadelphia: John C. Winston, 1929).

SAM KEEN is a psychologist who holds a Th.M. from the Harvard Divinity School and a Ph.D. from

Princeton University. "Maturity involves . . ." (p. 90) from *Inward Bound: Exploring the Geography of your Emotions* (New York: Bantam Books, 1992); "If I answer the appeal . . ." (p. 109), "To love is . . ." (p. 111) from *The Passionate Life: Stages of Loving* (New York: HarperCollins, 1984).

J. KRISHNAMURTI (1895–1986), an Indian philosopher educated in England, traveled the world teaching and advocating a way of life and thought unconditioned by the limitations of nationality, race, and religion. "Put away the book . . ." (p. 73) from *Commentaries on Living: Third Series* (Wheaton, Ill.: The Theosophical Publishing House, 1967); "Have we actually . . ." (p. 82) from *Talks to American Students* (Boston: Shambhala Publications, 1970); "We want to be sure . . ." (p. 96) from *Commentaries on Living;* "It had been a cool day . . ." (p. 115) from *Krishnamurti's Notebook* (New York: Harper & Row, 1976); "Love is an extraordinary thing . . ." (p. 117) from *Commentaries on Living.*

D. H. LAWRENCE (1885–1930) was an English novelist, poet, and essayist known for his attempt to interpret human emotion on a deep level of consciousness. "Love is a relationship . . ." (p. 2), "You can't worship love . . ." (p. 50) from "Love Was Once a Little Boy," "So it is with life . . ." (p. 138) from "Do Women Change?"

in *Phoenix II: Uncollected, Unpublished, and Other Prose Works* (New York: Viking Press, 1968).

STEPHEN LEVINE is internationally known for his workshops and books on meditation, healing, and grief work. He and his wife, Ondrea Levine, have served the terminally ill since 1980 as codirectors of the Hanuman Foundation Dying Project. "When we speak of love . . ." (p. 9), "The essential love . . ." (p. 110), "Love is the last element . . ." (p. 139) from *Healing into Life and Death* (New York: Anchor Books, 1987).

C. S. LEWIS (1898–1963), an Irish-born academic, writer, and Christian apologist, is well known for his science fiction and children's books. His brief but happy marriage to the poet Joy Davidman is portrayed in the film *Shadowlands.* "To love at all . . ." (p. 59) from *The Four Loves* (London: William Collins, 1960).

ANNE MORROW LINDBERGH is a writer best known for her book *Gift from the Sea,* which reflects a lifelong relationship with islands and the sea: time spent in Maine when she was a young girl, early married life on an island off the coast of Brittany, and retirement on Maui until the death of her husband, the aviator Charles Lindbergh. "A good relationship . . ." (p. 80), "Security in a relationship . . ." (p. 97), "One learns to accept . . ."

(p. 105) from *Gift from the Sea* (New York: Vintage Books, 1955).

CARSON McCULLERS (1917–1967), born in Georgia, is credited with fashioning the "Southern Gothic." Her novels are peopled with grotesque characters who reflect normal, universal human problems. "First of all, love is . . ." (p. 14), "Most of us . . ." (p. 45) from *The Ballad of the Sad Café and Other Stories* (New York: Bantam Books, 1991).

ABRAHAM MASLOW (1908–1970) was a pioneer in what has come to be known as humanistic psychology. He claimed that humans have two sets of needs: basic needs like food and security, and "metaneeds" like justice, unity, and love. "The confrontation with death . . ." (p. 92) from a letter to Rollo May quoted in *Love and Will* (New York: W. W. Norton, 1969).

ROLLO MAY is a practitioner of existentialist psychotherapy known for his eclectic sources of knowledge, insight, and example. "Eros is the drive . . ." (p. 42), "To love means . . ." (p. 56), "Love grows in depth . . ." (p. 65), "Sex is saved . . ." (p. 87), "To love . . ." (p. 130) from *Love and Will* (New York: W. W. Norton, 1969).

THOMAS MOORE, Ph.D., is a psychotherapist and writer who lived as a monk in a Catholic religious order for twelve years. "A soulful relationship . . ." (p. 72), "We often assume . . ." (p. 100), "Relationship is not only . . ." (p. 128) from *SoulMates: Honoring the Mysteries of Love and Relationship* (New York: HarperCollins, 1994).

IRIS MURDOCH is an Irish novelist and philosopher whose works focus on the relationships between art and philosophy, love and freedom, knowledge and morality. "Man's creative struggle . . ." (p. 22) from *The Black Prince* (New York: Viking Press, 1973); "Love is the extremely difficult . . ." (p. 30) from "The Sublime and the Good" (essay in *The Chicago Review* 13, 1959); "When sexual desire . . ." (p. 41), "How to convey . . ." (p. 81), "The foreverness of real love . . ." (p. 112) from *The Black Prince.*

HUA-CHING NI is a Taoist meditation master and natural healer from China who teaches at the Shrine of the Eternal Breath of Tao in Santa Monica, California. "Love is a very important matter . . ." (p. 6), "Love can be fulfilled . . ." (p. 83), "When the time comes . . ." (p. 119) from *I Ching: The Book of Changes and the Unchanging Truth* (Santa Monica, Calif.: Shrine of the Eternal Breath of Tao, 1983).

ANAÏS NIN (1903–1977), an American writer born in Paris, studied psychoanalysis under Otto Rank. She is best known for her friendships with other well-known artists and writers (chronicled in the seven volumes of her journals) and for her influence on feminism. "We both started . . ." (p. 62), "One always loves . . ." (p. 77) from *The Diary of Anaïs Nin: Volume One* (New York: Holt, Rhinehart & Winston, 1966).

A. R. ORAGE (1873–1934), an English editor and social thinker, lectured on behalf of G. I. Gurdjieff. "Love is for creation . . ." (p. 21), "Take hold tightly . . ." (p. 93) from *On Love* (London: Unicorn Press, 1932).

P. D. OUSPENSKY (1878–1947) was a Russian philosopher who, under the influence of G. I. Gurdjieff, devoted himself to the study of practical methods of developing human consciousness. Born in Moscow, he lived and taught in England and the United States following the Russian Revolution. "In reality love is . . ." (p. 5), "In all living nature . . ." (p. 23), "Love unfolds . . ." (p. 61), "Love in relation . . ." (p. 134) from *Tertium Organum* (London: Routledge & Kegan Paul, 1965).

SAINT PAUL (1st century), the Apostle of the Gentiles, was a rabbi and tentmaker. Until a vision of Jesus Christ converted him into a fervent adherent of the new faith, he assisted in persecuting Christians. "I may speak in tongues . . ." (p. 123) from 1 Cor. 13 in *The New English Bible* (New York: Oxford University Press, 1972).

PLATO (c. 428 BCE–c. 348 BCE), the pupil of Socrates and the teacher of Aristotle, is considered one of the most important philosophers of all time. "Love . . . is . . ." (p. 4), "Love seems to me . . ." (p. 12), "Yes, Love, who showers . . ." (p. 46), "What is most admirable . . ." (p. 121), "Love walks not . . ." (p. 126), "Love interprets . . ." (p. 135) from "The Symposium," trans. Percy Bysshe Shelley, in *Five Dialogues* (London: J. M. Dent, 1910).

JACQUES PRÉVERT (1900–1977) was a French poet and screenwriter associated with the Surrealist movement in the 1920s. "Love is . . ." (p. 15) *Children of Paradise* (New York: Simon & Schuster, 1968).

MARCEL PROUST (1871–1922), the French novelist, confined himself to a sound-proof flat and gave himself over entirely to introspection after his mother died when he was thirty-four. His thirteen-volume work *Remembrance of Things Past* was the result. "Since desire . . ." (p. 63) quoted in *The Diary of Anaïs Nin: Volume One* (New York: Holt, Rhinehart and Winston); "With every occurrence . . ." (p. 127), "As by an electric current . . ." (p. 133) from *Remembrance of Things Past,* trans. C. K. Scott Moncrieff and Terence Kilmartin (New York: Random House, 1981).

RAINER MARIA RILKE (1875–1926) was a Czech-born lyric poet whose work extended the range of expression and subtlety of the German language. He was married to a pupil of Rodin, whose secretary Rilke became in Paris. "For one human being . . ." (p. 47) from *Letters to a Young Poet,* trans. Stephen Mitchell (New York: Random House, 1984); "A complete sharing . . ." (p. 52) from *Letters of Rainer Maria Rilke,* trans. Jane Bannard Greene and M. D. Herter Norton (New York: W. W. Norton, 1945); "Love consists . . ." (p. 68) from *Letters to a Young Poet.*

BERTRAND RUSSELL (1872–1970) was a Welsh philosopher and mathematician, a prolific author, and a controversial public figure. "To fear love . . ." (p. 57) from *Marriage and Morals* (New York: Liveright, 1970); "Of all forms of caution . . ." (p. 60) from *The Conquest of Happiness* (New York: Liveright, 1958).

ANTOINE DE SAINT-EXUPÉRY (1900–1944), French novelist and airman, is best known for writing *The Little Prince.* "Love is not . . ." (p. 49) from *Wind, Sand and Stars,* trans. Lewis Galàntière (London: Heinemann, 1954).

MAY SARTON is an American poet and novelist whose search for inner truth is chronicled in her journals. "Because passionate love . . ." (p. 54) from *Recovering: A Journal* (New York: W. W. Norton, 1987); "The people we love . . ." (p. 64), " 'Loneliness' for me . . ." (p. 69) from

The House by the Sea (New York: W. W. Norton, 1981): "How unnatural the imposed view . . ." (p. 91) from *Journal of a Solitude* (New York: W. W. Norton, 1992); "Sunlight pours . . ." (p. 104) from *Plant Dreaming Deep* (New York: W. W. Norton, 1984).

WILLIAM SHAKESPEARE (1564–1616) the celebrated English playwright, was also a poet, actor, joint-manager of a London acting company, and part-owner of one of its theaters. His works have been popular from the moment he wrote them. "Love comforteth . . ." (p. 108) from *Venus and Adonis*.

STENDHAL, pseudonym of Henri Marie Beyle (1783–1842), was a French novelist, journalist, and diplomat who also wrote books on art and music. "The sight of anything . . ." (p. 25), "Let a lover's mind . . ." (p. 28), trans. John Sell from *De l'amour* (Lausanne: La Guilde de Livre, 1966).

RABINDRANATH TAGORE (1861–1941), Bengali poet and philosopher, was born in Calcutta and studied law in England. He received the Nobel Prize for Literature in 1913. His works include *Binodini,* considered to be the first truly modern novel by an Indian writer. "What in common language . . ." (p. 26), "Love is not . . ." (p. 67), from *A Tagore Reader* (New York: Macmillan, 1961).

PIERRE TEILHARD DE CHARDIN (1881–1955) was a French Jesuit theologian, paleontologist, and philosopher. His research in paleontology did not conform to Jesuit orthodoxy and his religious superiors forbade him to teach or publish. However, he won academic awards for his work. His philosphical speculations, rooted in his scientific work, were published posthumously. "Love is the most universal . . ." (p. 3), "Love is a sacred reserve . . ." (p. 7) from *Let Me Explain* (London: Collins, 1970); "Driven by the forces of love . . ." (p. 20), "There is but one . . ." (p. 31), "Even under the irresistible . . ." (p. 35), "To love is . . ." (p. 43) from *The Future of Man* (New York: Harper & Row, 1964); "At what moment . . ." (p. 114) from *The Phenomenon of Man* (New York: Harper & Row, 1959).

LEO TOLSTOY (1828–1910), the famous Russian novelist, was also an aesthetic philosopher, moralist, and mystic. His conflicted relationship with his wife has been the subject of several books. "Love is life . . ." (p. 141) from *War and Peace,* trans. Constance Garnett (New York: Random House, 1979).

CHÖGYAM TRUNGPA (1939–1987), a Tibetan Buddhist meditation master, scholar, poet, and artist, taught in North America from 1970 until his death. "In order to develop love . . ." (p. 55) from *Cutting Through Spiritual Materialism* (Boston: Shambhala Publications,

1987); "The idea of relationship . . ." (p. 101) from *The Heart of the Buddha* (Boston: Shambhala Publications, 1990); "Free passion is radiation . . ." (p. 113) from *The Myth of Freedom and the Way of Meditation* (Boston: Shambhala Publications, 1976).

VIRGIL (70–19 BCE) was a Roman poet whose works were established classics in his own lifetime and have remained so ever since. "Love conquers . . ." (p. 122) from The *Eclogues,* trans. Robert Coleman (New York: Cambridge University Press, 1979).

VIVEKANANDA (1863–1902) was the chief disciple of the great spiritual master Ramakrishna. He spent four years teaching in the West and founded two societies in New York and San Francisco. "The unity of all . . ." (p. 38) from *Living at the Source: Yoga Teachings of Vivekananda* (Boston: Shambhala Publications, 1993).

ALAN WATTS (1915–1973) was an English-born American philosopher whose books and lectures on Zen and Taoism popularized Eastern thought in the West. "Love brings the real . . ." (p. 29), "Above all, sexual love . . ." (p. 40) from *Nature, Man, and Woman* (New York: Pantheon Books, 1958); "Interestingly, we say 'falling' . . ." (p. 94) from *Play to Live* (South Bend, Ind.: And Books, 1982); "The height of sexual love . . ."

(p. 129) from *Nature, Man, and Woman;* "Is it only when . . ." (p. 132) from *Play to Live.*

JOHN WELWOOD, Ph.D., is a psychotherapist, a teacher, and a writer on topics such as meditation and relationships. "In the co-emergence of love and fear . . ." (p. 58), "Great love . . ." (p. 66), from *Journey of the Heart: Intimate Relationship and the Path of Love* (New York: HarperCollins, 1990).

MARION WOODMAN is a Toronto-based Jungian analyst who is internationally known as a teacher, lecturer, workshop leader, and author. "Relationship, as I understand it . . ." (p. 84), "It seems to me . . ." (p. 99) from *The Pregnant Virgin: A Process of Psychological Transformation* (Toronto: Inner City Books, 1985); "So long as we are concretizing . . ." (p. 102) from *Addiction to Perfection: The Still Unravished Bride* (Toronto: Inner City Books, 1982); "I think there's a dimension . . ." (p. 107) from *Conscious Femininity: Interviews with Marion Woodman* (Toronto: Inner City Books, 1993).

VIRGINIA WOOLF (1882–1941), the English novelist, critic, and essayist, is regarded as one of the great innovators of the modern English novel. "Directly one looked up . . ." (p. 16) from *To the Lighthouse* (London: The Hogarth Press, 1927).

DHYANI YWAHOO is a member of the traditional Etowah Band of the Eastern Tsalagi (Cherokee) Nation and the twenty-seventh generation to carry the ancestral wisdom of the Ywahoo lineage. She is the founder of Sunray Meditation Society in Bristol, Vermont. "Practice of sacred relationship . . ." (p. 79), "Be courageous . . ." (p. 86), "Know that all . . ." (p. 137) from *Voices of Our Ancestors* (Boston: Shambhala Publications, 1987).

CREDITS

ABOUT THE EDITOR

EMILY HILBURN SELL is an editor who has worked with many popular authors, including Marion Woodman, Linda Leonard, Natalie Goldberg, Peter Matthiessen, Maureen Murdoch, Chögyam Trungpa, Pema Chödrön, and John Welwood. Her translation of *Prometheus Bound* has been anthologized in *The Tenth Muse: Classical Drama in Translation.* She lives with her husband and son in Halifax, Nova Scotia.